LOOKING BACK
AT
MANCHESTER

CHRIS MAKEPEACE

Willow
PUBLISHING

Willow Publishing 1988
Willow Cottage, 36 Moss Lane,
Timperley, Altrincham,
Cheshire, WA15 6SZ.

© Chris Makepeace 1988

Reprinted 1993

ISBN 0 946361 24 X

Printed by the Commercial
Centre Ltd., Clowes Street,
Hollinwood, Oldham

Cross Street – Newall's Buildings

Newall's Buildings stood at the corner of Cross Street and Market Street. When it
was built in 1833 it was described as a fine stone structure. Its owner was William
Newall, a tea merchant and grocer, who had acquired the site in 1830 for £7,500.
The building had shops at street level, a large meeting room and smaller committee
room on the first floor and a circulating library on the top floor. It was from
Newall's Buildings that the Anti-Corn Law League was directed during the late
1830's and 1840's. Newall's Buildings was demolished in 1866 prior to the
rebuilding of an enlarged Royal Exchange.

Royal Exchange

INTRODUCTION

Change is essential if a city is to develop and move with the times. However, there are periods when the speed of change appears to be more rapid and more destructive than at others. One such period in Manchester's development is the last twenty or so years when the Arndale Centre and the Market Place redevelopment resulted in the wholesale clearance of a large area between Market Street, Deansgate, Shudehill and High Street. Other redevelopment that has occurred has been the result of infilling sites where the buildings were destroyed in the blitz or where buildings have been claimed to have outlived their usefulness and replaced by modern development structures. Some of this redevelopment has removed buildings of little architectural merit, but in some cases, fine buildings have been lost and the only visible record is through the photograph. One result of this increased pace of rebuilding is that the average person tends to feel insecure as familiar landmarks and friendly buildings disappear and are replaced by impersonal tower blocks and monolithic centres. This insecurity appears to have encouraged people to take an interest in what their city was like before the changes started, to look back, possibly through rose-coloured spectacles, at what they remember as the "good old days", forgetting the myriad problems, poor conditions and lack of modern facilities.

"Vanished Manchester" attempts to show some of the main streets in central Manchester where there have been many changes since 1945. However, there are illustrations of streets where the changes have been fewer and it is possible to recognise buildings in the photographs. Needless to say, certain streets and areas have been covered in greater detail than others. It is hoped the book will appeal not only to Mancunians, both young and old, but also to visitors to the city who want to know what the city looked like before the modern changes took place, and at the same time learn a little about the history of the streets and buildings. The photographs cover a period of roughly 100 years, from about 1860 to 1960 and are presented in the form of a walk. Thus, it is possible to follow the pictures and see what is still there today.

I should like to thank the Publisher for the opportunity to present this picture of Manchester's changing face. Also David Brearley for making copies of the illustrations, the staff of Manchester Local History Library for getting material from the stacks. My grateful thanks are also owed to all those Mancunians and others who have passed on information which has helped with my understanding of and knowledge about Manchester. Finally, I must thank my wife, Hilary, for her encouragement and advice whilst working on the book and Peter and Anna for tolerating their father's preoccupation with collecting information on Manchester and writing about the city.

Victoria Station

Victoria Station, built by the Manchester and Leeds Railway (later the Lancashire and Yorkshire Railway), was opened in 1844. The original station was designed by Robert Stephenson, and is the two-storey block with chimneys on the left of the photograph of Hunts Bank, taken in 1878. The station was also used by the London and North Western Railway until 1884 when it moved to Exchange Station. As the level of rail traffic increased in the latter half of the 19th century, Victoria Station was extended to meet the rapidly increasing demands made on its facilities. To the right can be seen the offices of the Lancashire and Yorkshire Railway, which were demolished in the late 1970's, and the entrance to Walkers Croft.

Long Millgate – Fish Dock Site

In 1901, the Lancashire and Yorkshire Railway Company embarked on a major expansion of the Long Millgate side of Victoria Station. In addition to a station roof, platforms and the removal of the old Cheetham Hill Road Bridge, a fish yard was created adjacent to Long Millgate. This work was completed and formally opened in 1904. In order to construct the fish yard, the buildings shown in this photograph, some of which date from the 18th century, had to be demolished. This photograph was taken about 1892 and shows the use of the buildings at that time. During the First World War, the fish platforms were used by troop trains.

Long Millgate – School Mills

Underneath Victoria Station flows the lower reaches of the River Irk, which is culverted from Ducie Bridge until it reaches the River Irwell. This photograph, dating from the mid 1860's, shows some of the mills on the banks of the Irk, the sites of which are now covered by Victoria Station. The mill in the centre was formerly owned by Manchester Grammar School, the income from which helped to pay for the costs of running the school.

Long Millgate – Manchester Arms

A notable Manchester building which has disappeared during the last decade is the Manchester Arms, which was sited on Long Millgate, close to the entrance to Victoria Station. This early 18th century building was originally the house of the Haworth family until 1788 when they sold it and it became a public house. It was from the garden of this building that the first balloon ascent in Manchester took place in 1785. It was sold in 1788 and converted to an inn, from which a coach ran three times a week to Bury. The main entrance to the Manchester Arms was on Long Millgate and not Corporation Street, as the latter was only constructed in the mid 19th century.

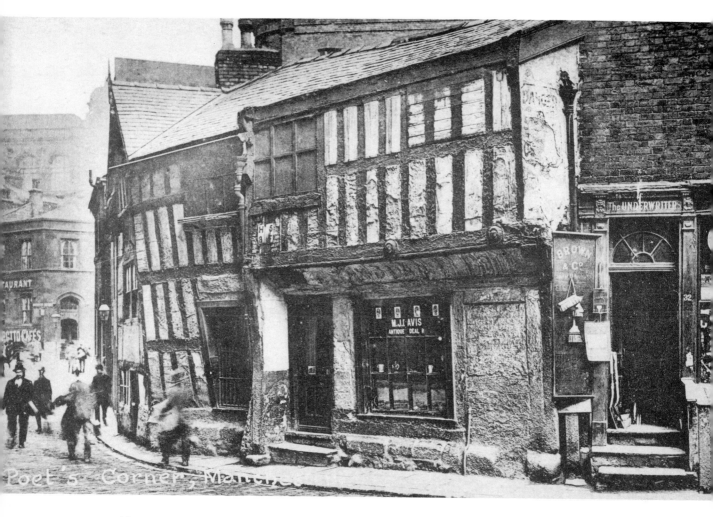

Poet's Corner, Manch...

Long Millgate – Poet's Corner

The Sun Inn, on the right of this photograph, was the venue for a small informal gathering of local poets and authors in the early 1840's. In 1842, the meetings became more frequent and continued until the licensee, William Earnshaw, moved in 1843. The results of these meetings were commemorated in a publication entitled "The Festive Wreath", as well as in the section of Long Millgate close to the Sun Inn being unofficially called Poet's Corner.

The Sun Inn was a half-timber building which had the date 1612 in one room, which may have been when alterations were made to the building. It continued as a public house until the mid 1860's when it lost its license. The building continued to stand until the 1920's when it was demolished as it had become unsafe.

Long Millgate – Chetham's

Sandwiched between Long Millgate, Victoria Station Approach, Hunts Bank,
Victoria Street and Fennel Street from 1653 until 1931 were two of Manchester's
major education establishments: Chetham's College and Manchester Grammar
School. Manchester Grammar School, founded in 1515, occupied the large block
on the right of the illustration together with other buildings closer to Hunts Bank.
The school was established by Hugh Oldham, Bishop of Exeter, and until 1865
was a free school. Fee-paying places were only introduced as a result of
competition from educational establishments and the need for the school to
expand its curriculum. Chetham's, which occupied the lower buildings around the
quadrangle in the photograph, was started in 1653 as a result of a bequest by
Humphrey Chetham which was given to the Collegiate Church in 1422 as a residence
for the clergy. The property was acquired by the Derby family in 1547, but was
confiscated during the Civil War. In addition to establishing a school, Chetham
also left money to establish a free library, which still exists today.

Lancaster Arcade

One of the earliest arcades to be constructed in Manchester was Lancaster Arcade, between Fennel Street and Todd Street. It was built of wood, cast iron and glass and had small shops on two levels. To some people it was reminiscent of a prison and there have been claims that it was once a women's prison, but this was not the case. It was a purpose-built arcade which was opened about 1853. In its latter years, it housed many small businesses, especially those involved with numismatics and jewellery. Unfortunately, Lancaster Arcade was demolished in the mid 1970's after years of neglect.

Shudehill/Withy Grove Market

This photograph shows a scene which has disappeared in Manchester, namely Shudehill market. In its latter years, it was well known as a book market, but when this photograph was taken, it was part of the Hen Market, which had moved to this area in the late 1860's after being displaced from the Market Place. Behind the ice-cream vendor can be seen part of the Rovers Return public house, a timber framed building which may have dated back to mediaeval times. It was demolished in 1957, almost forty years after the Seven Stars, another timber-framed public house in the area, had been demolished. Today, the land occupied by the buildings lies under the Arndale Bus Station.

Smithfield Market

During the 19th century, the various markets that existed in Manchester were
gradually centralised in the Smithfield area. This was speeded up after 1846 when
the borough council acquired the manorial rights from the Mosley family. Not
only were there the wholesale fish and fruit and vegetables markets, but also a
retail fish market and numerous out-door retail stalls. The wholesale markets have
now been moved from central Manchester and the remaining buildings have been
found other uses. With the disappearance of the wholesale markets, the stalls have
also gone, whilst the buildings which were used as stores and shops have acquired
a new lease of life through the work of members of the Asian community in
Manchester engaged in the clothing trade.

Cannon Street

One street which has changed beyond all recognition since 1945 is Cannon Street. This photograph was taken about 1920 from its junction with Corporation Street. All the buildings shown in the photograph have now disappeared, mainly as a result of the development of the Arndale Centre. It was along Cannon Street that many of the early textile warehouses were to be found in the early 19th century. However, Cannon Street continued to play an important role in the wholesale textile trade up to the latter half of the 20th century.

Hanging Ditch – Corn and Produce Exchange

The first Corn Exchange had been opened in 1837 in a building designed by Richard Lane, but by the late 19th century this had become inadequate for the demands made upon it. A new Exchange, designed by Ball and Elce, was built between 1893 and 1903, each wing of the building being opened as soon as it was completed. In the centre of the building, a large open floor was provided for traders to meet and transact business.

Victoria Street

When the Manchester Diocese was created in 1847, the Parish Church of Manchester, known as the Collegiate Church, became the Cathedral for the new diocese. This photograph of about 1889 shows Victoria Street passing the west end of the Cathedral. It was the construction of Victoria Street in the 1830's that removed that portion of the graveyard between the west end and the River Irwell. The porch at the west end which is to be seen today was added in 1897 to celebrate Queen Victoria's Diamond Jubilee. During the 19th century, the building underwent two major restorations, the second being to restore its mediaeval splendour. Behind the Cathedral can be seen Palatine Buildings and Chetham's College whilst to its right are the buildings, demolished about 1890, which resulted in the rediscovery of the mediaeval Hanging Bridge, part of which can still be seen today.

Victoria Street – Cromwell Statue and Exchange Station

In 1876 the Cromwell Monument was donated by Mrs. Abel Heywood in memory of her first husband, Alderman Goadsby. The statue, sited on an island close to the junction of Victoria Street and Deansgate, was regarded by some as a traffic hazard and by others as insensitive being so close to the Cathedral. In 1968 the statue was moved to Wythenshawe Park when redevelopment of the area commenced. Behind the statue is Exchange Station, opened in 1884 by the London and North Western Railway. Exchange Station was closed in 1969, on the same day as Central Station. The office block shown in this early 20th century photograph was destroyed in the Christmas blitz of 1940.

Victoria Bridge

Victoria Bridge was constructed between 1837 and 1839 as a replacement for the mediaeval old Salford Bridge, which stood on the same site. The bridge was the only toll-free crossing of the Irwell in central Manchester until 1803. Consequently it was always congested. Even the demolition of an old chantry chapel in 1788 and the widening of the approaches did little to relieve the situation. Floods and gales caused problems with the new bridge, but in March 1839, it was opened, having cost £20,800 to construct. To the right of the bridge, where the foundations of a new building are to be seen, was the site of Ben Lang's Music Hall where a false fire alarm in 1868 caused 24 deaths.

Old Millgate

Old Millgate ran from the Market Place to Cateaton Street and afforded a view of the east end of the Cathedral from the Market Place. Today, Old Millgate no longer exists, being lost under the new development in and around the Market Place. When this photograph was taken at the end of the 19th century, the buildings had a variety of uses. The ground floors were often shops whilst there were offices and workshops above. It is interesting to note that above the shop advertising its stock-taking sale were the rooms of the Central Exchange Billiard Club, and opposite was a skittle alley and shooting range. Although all the buildings on Long Millgate have disappeared, the Mitre Hotel, part of whose sign can be seen beyond the fencing, is still extant as a hotel.

Market Place – c.1860

The original Manchester Market Place no longer exists. The blitz destroyed many of the buildings and, with the exception of the Wellington Inn and Sinclair's Oyster Bar, the remainder were swept away by redevelopment in the 1970's. The original area called the Market Place now lies under Marks and Spencer's store. This photograph of the Market Place must have been taken prior to 1864 as it shows the Royal Exchange building, which was demolished in 1866, in the background, and Victoria Fish and Game Market, demolished in 1864, in the right-hand foreground. The Royal Exchange building was designed by Thomas Harrison of Chester and was granted the prefix "Royal" in 1851 after Queen Victoria's visit to Manchester.

Market Place – 1878

Until 1891, the shops in the Market place were dominated by the market stalls. In that year, the City Council decided to remove the stalls, which was greeted with approval in the local press. This photograph, by Alfred Brothers in 1878, shows the Market Place looking towards the Royal Exchange. It also shows the stalls which created so much congestion on market days as they blocked the road and made passage through the area difficult for both pedestrians and vehicles.

Market Place – Early 20th Century

This view of the Market Place was taken looking from Market Street towards the Cathedral. It clearly shows the narrowness of the Market Place as well as some of the buildings which surrounded it. It is possible that it did extend further towards the Cathedral as Yates's building is clearly dated "1826". Yates was a well known seedsman in the Manchester area and apparently planted Stanley Hall Wood at Disley as his nursery. Next door can be seen the Falstaff Hotel. To the right of the Wellington Inn is the building which replaced the Victoria fish and game market.

Market Place – Wellington Inn

The Wellington Inn and Sinclair's Oyster Bar are the only buildings of the pre-war Market Place which are still standing. This photograph of about 1860 shows the Wellington Inn, which dates from the 16th or early 17th centuries and which was originally a private house. It was not licensed until the 1830's. When this photograph was taken the upper floor was used by an optician, who advertised his profession in a spectacular way with a pair of large glasses. The redevelopment of the Market Place area forced the developers to raise the building up almost five feet to a new level. When the work was completed, the notice at first floor level was still in situ, but when the building was restored, this interesting piece of history unfortunately disappeared.

Market Place — Bull's Head Yard

Originally the Bull's Head Hotel faced onto the Market Place, but in the 19th century it sold its frontage onto the Market Place and made a new main entrance from the former stable yard. This 1930's photograph shows the entrance to the hotel which was created in the 19th century with its large bull's head over the door. It also shows a little of the other buildings in the area which appear to be Georgian in origin. The Bull's Head was destroyed in the Christmas blitz of 1940.

Smithy Door – Vintner's Arms

When the construction of Victoria Street was started in 1833, most of the mediaeval Smithy Door, adjacent to the Market Place, was swept away. How this area got its name is uncertain, but by the late 18th century it was used as an extension of the Market Place. This photograph, taken in 1875, shows the Vintner's Arms, the last remaining building in Smithy Door, just prior to its demolition to enable the erection of Victoria Buildings. The Vintner's Arms, or Deakin's Entire as it is sometimes described, was a timber-framed building about which nothing is known until 1800 when it was occupied by a Mr. Saunders, an Irish linen importer. It was first licensed in 1804, the licensee being Mrs. Wilmott, whose family was there for 40 years, after which a Mr. Sandiford took it over and renamed it the "Vintner's Arms".

St. Mary's Gate – Victoria Buildings

This photograph, taken in the 1890's, shows the St. Mary's Street elevation of Victoria Buildings, erected on the site of Smithy Door. The aim of the new building was to provide good shops near the Market Place. Victoria Buildings was designed by William Dawes and cost £140,000. In addition to the 31 shops fronting Deansgate, St. Mary's Gate and Victoria Street, there was also a covered shopping arcade. The new building, completed in 1878, included a large hotel overlooking the junction of Victoria Street and Deansgate. Amongst the architectural features Dawes included in the building were carvings of scenes from the fables of Aesop and Krelof, the columns between the shop windows showing scenes from Aesop's fables. Victoria Buildings was destroyed in the Christmas blitz of 1940.

St. Mary's Gate – Post War Victoria Buildings

After the Second World War, there were a number of bomb sites in the heart of Manchester including the site of Victoria Buildings. Until a scheme for the redevelopment of the site was agreed, the area was landscaped, as these 1950's photographs show. Its location in relation to the buildings which are there today can be seen by looking at Sinclair's Oyster Bar, which is the "black and white" building in the picture, to the left of the Royal Exchange tower.

Corporation Street

This photograph taken in the 1960's shows buildings on Corporation Street and Cross Street which were demolished to enable the Arndale Centre to be built. Corporation Street was not constructed until the 1840's when it was felt that a more direct route to Cheetham Hill Road (then known as York Street) was required. When Corporation Street was created, it sliced through the heart of the mediaeval Manchester around the Market Place, destroying not only old buildings but also the old street pattern.

Market Street – Bottom End

Market Street, originally known as Market Stede Lane, was the main road to the centre of Manchester from the south. Originally it was a narrow, irregular road lined with timber-framed houses, which were partly used for residential purposes and partly used as shops and warehouses. This photograph shows the junction of Market Street and the Market Place in 1902. The site of these buildings is now covered by Marks and Spencer's store.

Market Street – Cross Street Junction

During the last twenty years, the eastern side of Market Street has changed out of all recognition. Although the road was widened and new buildings erected between 1821 and 1833, alterations were continually made to the buildings until they assumed the appearance that they have in the photograph, taken in 1902. The buildings shown, at the junction of Cross Street, Market Street and Corporation Street have all been demolished and replaced by the Arndale Centre.

Market Street – Western Side

Although the eastern side of Market Street has radically changed in appearance, many of the buildings on the western side still remain, as this photograph taken in the 1890's shows. One difference that will be noticed is that the view of the tower on the Royal Exchange has now been obliterated by the bridge linking the two sections of the Arndale development, as have the buildings at the Cross Street end of this side of Market Street.

Market Street – Upper End

Market Street was one of Manchester's busiest streets which often suffered from
traffic congestion. As a result, in 1906 proposals were tabled to pedestrianise it, but
it was not undertaken until the 1980's. This photograph shows Market Street,
looking north, in 1930, and was taken near the junction of Tib Street and Market
Street. On the left is Lewis's store, and Rylands building is on the right. The
building to the left of the tram still stands today and may be one of the oldest
buildings still standing on Market Street, having been erected in the mid 19th
century.

Market Street/Piccadilly

This is the view which anyone walking from Piccadilly into Market Street would have had at the beginning of the 20th century. On the right is the Royal Hotel, built originally as a private house in 1772, and converted to a coaching inn and hotel in 1828. The Royal Hotel was demolished in 1908 and replaced by the present buildings. Beyond the Royal Hotel can be seen the tower of Lewis's store, the firm having established itself in Manchester around 1880. On the right is the White Bear Hotel, originally the town house of the Lever family of Alkrington, which was converted into a coaching inn in 1788. It was demolished in 1904 to make way for a Ceylon Tea House. The building opposite Lewis's was occupied by Rylands, one of Manchester's major textile firms.

Piccadilly – East Side

Piccadilly is one of the best known parts of central Manchester. Until about 1812, it was known as Lever's Row and was a popular residential area, especially with the medical profession due to its proximity to the Infirmary. During the 19th century, the area changed as commercial and business interests took over from private residents. This photograph shows the east side of Piccadilly in the mid 1890's. The white building on the corner of Oldham Street is the Albion Hotel, which was said to have had one of the best cuisines in Europe in the mid-19th century. It closed in 1926 and was replaced by a Woolworth's store. Many of the other buildings, however, are still there today.

Piccadilly – East Side 2

This view of Piccadilly was taken after the last war and shows some of the buildings which were on the previous photograph. The Woolworth's store is on the site of the Albion Hotel whilst the tall building next to it housed the BBC studios in Manchester. The photograph also clearly shows the Esplanade, which was created in 1853 on the site of the Daub Holes and was the location for a splendid fountain when Queen Victoria first visited Manchester in October 1851. The cost of creating the Esplanade was over £6000 although Thomas Worthington had prepared a scheme which could have cost only about £3500.

Piccadilly Infirmary

Piccadilly Gardens was originally the site of Manchester Royal Infirmary, established in 1752 in rented accommodation on Garden Street. In 1754, the Piccadilly site was acquired. The new Infirmary was opened in 1755. Throughout the 18th and 19th centuries, the buildings were enlarged several times to meet the growing demands made on its facilities. By the end of the 19th century, expansion and modernisation of the hospital was required, but this was not possible on the existing site. In 1902 a new site was acquired on Oxford Road. The new hospital was completed in 1908. The patients were transferred in December 1908, and the old buildings demolished in April 1910. This photograph, taken about 1909, shows the Infirmary's Portland Street façade which was similar to that on Mosley Street. The main façade on to Piccadilly also had a matching portico, which was surmounted by a dome and clock.

Piccadilly Gardens – Library Huts

When the Infirmary was demolished in 1910, there was much discussion as to the future use of the site. However, before any decision could be taken, it became essential to find a temporary home for Manchester Free Library as the former Town Hall on King Street had become too dangerous to use. As a temporary measure, huts were erected on part of the Infirmary site to serve as a Reference Library until a new building could either be found or built for the library. This temporary measure lasted until the present Central Library in St. Peter's Square was opened in 1934. The photograph shows some of the huts that were there in 1929 and their position in Piccadilly Gardens.

PICCADILLY GARDENS, MANCHESTER

Piccadilly – Parker Street

This photograph of Piccadilly Gardens was taken in 1928 looking from the building which is now occupied by the Piccadilly branch of the National Westminster Bank. At that time the upper floors of the building housed the BBC in Manchester. Behind Piccadilly Gardens can be seen the warehouses on Parker Street which were destroyed during the 1940 Christmas blitz. Today, the site is occupied by the Piccadilly Plaza development.

Piccadilly – Parker Street

As a result of the blitz, a large area between Parker Street and York Street became
an open space which was used as a surface car park until the Piccadilly Plaza
development was started around 1960. This photograph, taken in 1957 from
Mosley Street, shows the car park and Parker Street Bus Station. In the
background is Watts Warehouse, to the left of which are warehouses, demolished
in the late 1960's, which stood where County Hall now stands. The new building
which replaced the warehouses was the headquarters of the Greater Manchester
County Council between 1974 and 1986. Behind the warehouses can be seen the
clock tower of the Minshull Street Police Courts, opened in 1873, designed by
Thomas Worthington.

Piccadilly – Queens Hotel

The Queen's Hotel stood at the corner of Piccadilly and Portland Street. It appears to have been a conversion by Edward Walters of a terrace of early 19th century town houses. It was William Houldsworth, nephew of the cotton magnate and race horse owner Thomas Houldsworth, who had lived in the corner property, who commissioned Walters to undertake the conversion. The hotel opened in 1852 and rapidly established itself as one of Manchester's leading hotels. In the late 19th century, The Queen's Hotel had a reputation for turtle soup which it supplied to other hotels and individual customers for private use. The hotel closed in the early 1970's and was demolished to be replaced by a modern office block.

Oldham Street

Oldham Street was created in 1772 to improve the road from New Cross into Manchester. It was named after Adam Oldham who owned land on the corner of what is now Piccadilly and Oldham Street. During the late 19th and early 20th centuries, Oldham Street was a fashionable shopping street with its many haberdashery stores. It was said that you could buy virtually everything you required from the cradle to the grave on Oldham Street. Although the buildings closest to Piccadilly, shown in this illustration, were impressive in their appearance, those nearer to New Cross were less attractive.

London Road Station

London Road Station (now Piccadilly Station) was opened in 1842 by the
Manchester and Birmingham Railway (later part of the London and North
Western Railway). By order of Parliament, the Manchester, Sheffield and
Lincolnshire Railway (later the Great Central Railway) also used the station, which
caused problems for a number of years after its opening. Between 1860 and 1866
the station was rebuilt and enlarged. The new buildings, designed by Mills and
Murgatroyd, were only demolished in the late 1950's under British Rail's
modernisation programme. This photograph, taken around 1910, shows the station
and its impressive location at the top of a short rise, one side of which was flanked
by warehouses of the Great Central Railway.

Portland Street – Watts Warehouse

Watts Warehouse, now the Britannia Hotel, was the grandest of the textile warehouses to be built in Manchester. It was designed by Travis and Mangnall and opened in March 1858. Each storey is said to be a different style of Renaissance architecture. The building cost almost £100,000, of which £30,000 was for the site. In 1892, the company employed 600 people in the warehouse and a further 300 on an adjacent site on Silver Street as well as 36 travellers. The stock, listed in a 384 page catalogue in 1892, was divided into 32 departments in such a way that orders could be quickly despatched. It was claimed that all orders received by the first post were dealt with on the day of receipt. To the right are some of the original early 19th century buildings which were soon to be demolished for new warehouse construction.

Portland Street

This photograph, taken in the late 1930's, shows the Piccadilly end of Portland Street. The building on the extreme right is Watts Warehouse and the warehouse next to it is where County Hall now stands. On the left are the warehouses which stood where Portland Street façade of Piccadilly Plaza is now to be seen. This photograph presents a very good impression of Manchester in the years before the Second World War, not only from the point of view of how the buildings looked, but also the atmosphere which prevailed.

Portland Street, 1920's

Portland Street was one of the main streets which passed through the textile warehouse area of Manchester. During the late 19th and early 20th centuries it was lined with tall warehouses, many in the distinctive Manchester palazzo style. The part of Portland Street shown in this 1920's illustration was created in the latter half of the 19th century when Portland Street cut through to a junction with Oxford Street. The warehouse on the right was built in the late 1860's, designed by P. Nunn and was partially occupied by the Behrens' family business.

Oxford Street

This illustration is taken from a coloured postcard and shows the Palace Theatre as it appeared about 1919. The Palace opened in 1891 as a variety theatre, which it continued to stage until the 1920's when full-length musicals started to be introduced. In 1913, the original building was remodelled internally and minor improvements were made to the exterior.

Oxford Street *(below and right)*

Oxford Street was started in 1792 to provide the villages to the south of Manchester with a better road into the centre of the city. This photograph, taken about 1937 from Central Library, shows the section of Oxford Street where almost all the buildings have now been demolished and replaced by modern buildings. Worthy of note is the second building on the right which was the Princes Theatre, one of a number of places of entertainment to be found along Oxford Street, Peter Street and Quay Street. It is also interesting to note that Oxford Street had two-way traffic at this point in time. The one-way system that operates today was not introduced until the following year.

St. Peter's Square – South Side

Almost all the buildings in this photograph of the south side of St. Peter's Square, taken about 1920, have now been demolished. Today, the only ones still standing are at the corner of Princess Street and Mosley Street and at the corner of Dickenson Street and Mosley Street, although this latter has been refurbished. If the buildings are studied carefully, it will be seen that the chimneys are on the outer wall of the buildings, a feature insisted upon by insurance companies to reduce the risk of fire in textile warehouses. In the centre of the traffic island is the stone cross commemorating the site of St. Peter's Church, but note that the Cenotaph has not yet been erected.

St. Peter's Square – Library Site

One of the best known buildings in central Manchester is the Central Library. However, this building was only opened in 1934. In order that the library might be built, the buildings shown in this illustration, which had been erected in the middle of the 19th century, had to be demolished. Their main use prior to their demolition in 1926 was as offices for professional firms such as solicitors, insurance brokers and textile merchants, whilst the ground floors tended to be used for commercial purposes such as cafés and by tailors.

St. Peter's Church

St. Peter's Church stood in the centre of St. Peter's Square on an island site where the Cenotaph is now located. It was designed by James Wyatt and opened in 1794. The tower was added in 1816 and was a feature which did not please Wyatt. The church was demolished in 1907 when most of the population in the area had moved away, as central Manchester had become a commercial rather than a residential area. A stone cross in the centre of the island commemorates the church's site today.

Mosley Street

Mosley Street came into existence in the late 18th century as Manchester started to expand rapidly from its core around the Market Place. It was one of a number of streets in central Manchester named after the Mosley family, who were Lords of the Manor. This photograph, taken in the early 20th century, shows the Art Gallery, designed by Sir Charles Barry in 1825 for the Royal Manchester Institution. The building and its collections were given to Manchester City Council in 1888. Beyond the Art Gallery can be seen the premises of the Union Club, founded in 1825. The building was designed by Richard Lane in 1834.

George Street – St. James's Church

St. James' Church, George Street, was opened in 1788 to serve the growing population around Piccadilly. It was quite a fashionable church, but during the 19th century, the wealthier members of the congregation moved away and it became a poor parish, sparsely attended. The church was closed and demolished in 1928. A multi-storey office block, called St. James's House, now stands on the site of the church, whilst the Bank of England building stands over part of the graveyard.

Central Station

Central Station, opened in July 1880, was built by the Cheshire Lines Committee as its Manchester terminus. The main feature of the station was the 210 feet single span cast-iron and glass roof. The original plans for the station included either offices or a hotel at the front, but were never implemented. Central Station was one of the busiest in the country with an extensive commuter traffic from areas to the south and west of Manchester and services to many parts of the country. One service which had a high reputation for speed and punctuality was that to Liverpool, which took only 43 minutes. Central Station closed in May 1969 and after many years of neglect, it was purchased by the Greater Manchester Council, who, in partnership with Commercial Union, restored the structure and converted it into the G-MEX exhibition centre.

Peter Street – Midland Hotel

The Midland Hotel, designed by George Trubshaw, was built by the Midland
Railway as the end of its line between London and Manchester on the site of the
Gentlemen's Concert Hall, the People's Concert Hall and Lower Mosley Street
Schools. Started in 1898, it was opened in 1904 and rapidly became the leading
hotel in the city. Amongst its facilities were banqueting rooms, a concert roof and
a roof garden together with electric lighting and facilities which enabled reservations
to be made from mid-Atlantic.

Peter Street – Free Trade Hall

The Free Trade Hall, designed by Edward Walters, was opened in 1856. It was built to commemorate the success of the Manchester based Anti-Corn Law League in securing the repeal of the corn laws, which controlled the import of grain into the United Kingdom. When it opened, it was the first public hall in Manchester which could be hired irrespective of the political, religious or social views held by the organisers of the event. This photograph, taken during May 1899, shows the canopy which allowed people attending events in the Free Trade Hall to reach the building from their carriages without getting wet.

Albert Square

Albert Square was created in the early 1860's to provide a suitable place to locate the Albert Memorial. To the right of the statue of John Bright can be seen the fountain erected in 1894 to commemorate the opening of the Thirlmere Aqueduct. The building that can be seen between the statue and the fountain is Princes Tavern, where Thomas de Quincey was born and lived at the end of the 18th century. The tall building on the right of the photograph is contemporary with the Town Hall, being completed in 1877. This photograph must have been taken in the late 1890's as the Princes Tavern was demolished around 1902.

Albert Square

This photograph shows Albert Square in the early 1930's. Central to the photograph is the Albert Memorial, erected in 1867. Also visible are the statues of Bright, Heywood and Gladstone. On the left are warehouses which were demolished in the 1970's. Just missing from the photograph on the extreme left is the building which housed Blacklocks, the publishers of Bradshaw's Railway Guide.

King Street – Old Town Hall

Manchester's original Town Hall was built by the Police Commissioners on the
site of Dr. Charles White's house on the corner of Cross Street and King Street
between 1822 and 1825. It was designed by Francis Goodwin and cost £25,000.
When the new Town Hall in Albert Square was opened in 1877, the redundant
building was converted so it could be used as the reference library section of the
Manchester Free Libraries. The library continued to use the building until 1912
when it was found to be dangerous and demolished. The columns from the front
portico, however, were preserved and re-erected by the lake in Heaton Park.

King Street – Banking Area

This photograph of the upper part of King Street was taken in the early 1960's and shows the buildings which stood where the National Westminster Bank and Pall Mall Court are now. The building occupied by the Vulcan Insurance Company was designed for the Royal Insurance Company in 1862 by Alfred Waterhouse, whilst the building adjacent to the tower was designed by Mills and Murgatroyd in 1889 for the Manchester and County Bank. This site was occupied in the first half of the 19th century by the York Hotel, where the borough council held its early meetings. The white building beyond the tower is Lloyds Bank, which stands on the site of the original Manchester Town Hall.

King Street – Lower Section

Although there has been no new building undertaken on the part of King Street between Cross Street and Deansgate in the last half century, the shop fronts have been considerably altered. The pedestrianisation of this part of King Street has made it possible to stroll along this attractive street of Victorian buildings and admire its architecture, especially that of No.35, which dates from about 1735 when it was a gentleman's residence. It is now used as a bank. This photograph, taken in November 1931, shows King Street at a time when parking was allowed on one side of the road, which alternated from side to side according to the date.

Cross Street – Cross Street Chapel

This photograph shows Cross Street Chapel before it was destroyed in the
Christmas blitz of 1940. The Chapel had been established for the Rev. Henry
Newcombe in 1694. In 1715 it was severely damaged by rioters, but was rebuilt
with government assistance. During the 19th century it was added to and was
described on one occasion as the "best brick built building in Manchester".
Originally it was a Presbyterian Chapel, but during the 18th century it became
connected with the Unitarian movement. Many of Manchester's leading citizens
were members of the congregation in the late 18th and early 19th centuries. The
chapel was also used as a meeting place for several organisations until they
established their own premises, amongst them being the Manchester Literary and
Philosophical Society and the Mechanics Institute.

Cross Street – Manchester Guardian Offices

For 130 years, the "Manchester Guardian" occupied the same site on Cross Street, opposite the Royal Exchange. The building shown in this photograph of 1902 was designed by Barker and Ellis between 1881 and 1886. When the building was opened it included the latest rotary presses for printing the newspaper. The "Manchester Guardian", famed for its liberal approach, was founded in 1821 by John Edward Taylor, and was first published from premises on Market Street, but about 1840 it moved to where it remained until 1970. In the 19th century, several newspapers were published in this area. For instance, in 1864, the first issue of the "Manchester City News" was published from an office on the site later to be incorporated within the Manchester Guardian's site. Four years later, in 1868 the "Manchester Evening News" was published and shortly afterwards it was sold to the "Manchester Guardian" as its founder had no further use for the evening paper.

Cross Street – Royal Exchange

An exchange has occupied the site of the present Royal Exchange building since work started on the construction of the Commercial Room in 1806. The building shown in this early 20th century photograph was designed by Mills and Murgatroyd and erected between 1866 and 1874 to cater for and accommodate a rapidly growing membership. The portico shown in the illustration faced Cross Street and was demolished before the First World War as part of a deal with the City Council enabling the Exchange to enlarge its premises, and the Council to widen Cross Street. The original use of the building ceased in 1968 due to the continuing decline of the British cotton industry.

ROYAL EXCHANGE, MANCHESTER.

Exchange Street

Exchange Street was constructed in 1788 to improve the access between St. Ann's Square and St. Mary's Gate/Market Street. The new street was in direct contrast to the narrow passage which had previously been the only means of access to St. Ann's Square from this part of Manchester. The photograph, taken about 1913, shows Exchange Street looking towards the Market Street/Victoria Street corner, which was the subject of the earliest known photograph of Manchester dating from 1842. On the left of the photograph are the offices of the Lancashire Insurance Company, designed by Thomas Turner in 1866. On the right is the Royal Exchange before its extension in 1919.

Albert Square – Town Hall

Manchester's magnificent Victorian Gothic Town Hall was built between 1868 and 1877 to the designs of Alfred Waterhouse. The new building was erected on a triangular shaped site which had formerly been the Town Yard. The new building, which cost £1m was opened in September 1877 by the Mayor, Alderman Abel Heywood after Queen Victoria had declined the invitation. The opening was followed by three days of celebrations, culminating in a Grand Trades Procession, which was reviewed by the Mayor.

Deansgate – Barton Buildings

This view of Deansgate in the early 20th century shows Barton Buildings, which includes the splendid Barton Arcade. The building was designed by Corbett, Raby and Sawyer and was completed in 1871. The building was erected as a result of a decision by Manchester to widen the south side of Deansgate which necessitated the demolition of the existing buildings between St. Mary's Gate and Peter Street.

St. Mary's Parsonage – St. Mary's Church

Between Deansgate and the Parsonage, close to Kendal's store, is a small landscaped area. This is the site of St. Mary's Church, opened in 1756, closed and demolished in 1888. Its design was based on that of Knutsford Parish Church. Originally it had a tower with a spire surmounted by a gilt ball and cross. The latter was taken down in 1823 as a result of storm damage, whilst the spire was demolished 31 years later as it was unsafe. When St. Mary's was closed its congregation was very small as most of the residents in the area had been forced to move further out of the centre of Manchester due to the pressures exerted by commercial development.